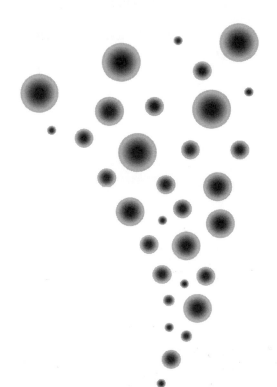

Get Back, Pimple!

Also by John Agard

LAUGHTER IS AN EGG
NO HICKORY, NO DICKORY, NO DOCK

2

Get Back, Pimple!

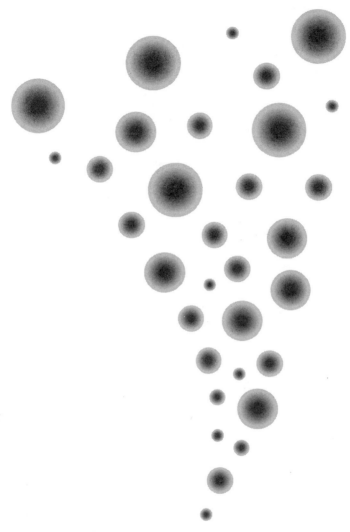

John Agard

Illustrated by the Point

VIKING

VIKING

Published by the Penguin Group
Penguin Books Ltd, 27 Wrights Lane, London W8 5TZ, England
Penguin Books USA Inc., 375 Hudson Street, New York, New York 10014, USA
Penguin Books Australia Ltd, Ringwood, Victoria, Australia
Penguin Books Canada Ltd, 10 Alcorn Avenue, Toronto, Ontario, Canada M4V 3B2
Penguin Books (NZ) Ltd, 182–190 Wairau Road, Auckland 10, New Zealand

Penguin Books Ltd, Registered Offices: Harmondsworth, Middlesex, England

First published 1996
1 3 5 7 9 10 8 6 4 2

Text copyright © John Agard, 1996
Illustrations copyright © the Point, 1996

The moral right of the author has been asserted

Filmset in Humanist 521

Made and printed in Great Britain by Butler & Tanner Ltd, Frome and London

A CIP catalogue record for this book is available from the British Library

ISBN 0–670–86198–7

4

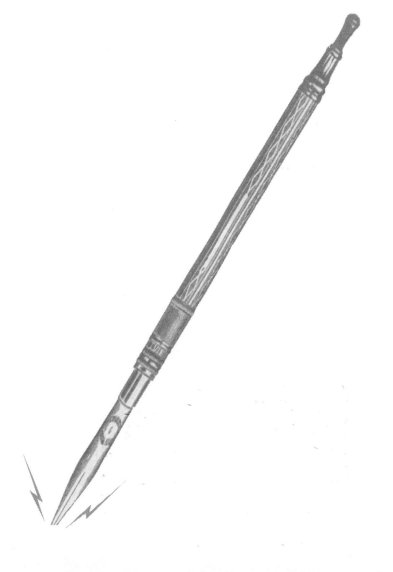

Contents

Tidy Up With Music

When Light and Shadow

I'd Like to Squeeze

God in Blue Denims

8

For Yansan & Lesley

who passed through a phase
of The Beastie Boys
& The Fat Boys
when teenage fears & joys
walked side by side.

May your dreams come true.

Love
Dad

Tidy Up With Music

Exams Blues

Wake up this morning can't find my pen
Wake up this morning can't find my pen
Exams driving me round the bend

History hollering round my head
History hollering round my head
Them kings and queens just won't stay dead

Never been one to toe the line
Never been one to toe the line
But maths done squared this head of mine

Physics turn me upside-down
Physics turn me upside-down
Can't tell no molecule from atom

But French I got news
French hear my news
Gonna parlez-vous in my dancing shoes

Not-Enough-Pocket-Money Blues

I could see myself stepping light and slow
in them jeans
so hip-sharp-tight and full-of-flow.
Could just ...
But I've got me the no-cash no-dosh
not-enough-pocket-money blues.

Could see myself slinking to school
in them trainers
so jaguar-sleek and puma-cool.
Could just ...
But I've got me the no-cash no-dosh
not-enough-pocket-money blues.

Could see myself a fashion queen
in that top
so flirty-smart and snazzy-sleeved.
Could just ...
But I've got me the no-cash no-dosh
not-enough-pocket-money blues.

Could see myself all summery
in that hat
so patchwork-wicked and flowery.
Could just ...
But I've got me the no-cash no-dosh
not-enough-pocket-money blues.

I guess I can always ask Mum.

Smoke-loving Girl Blues

Would like her for my girlfriend any day
Would follow if she showed the way
Would feel honoured if she be my queen

But she's a smoke-loving girl
And I'm allergic to nicotine

Would wheel with her on the ice-skating rink
Would fall with her over the brink
Would stare with her bewitched and serene

But she's a smoke-loving girl
And I'm allergic to nicotine

Would give her my last polo mint
Would hit the skies if she gave me a hint
Would do anything even dye my hair green

But she's a smoke-loving girl
And I'm allergic to nicotine

Would lay down my jacket for her gorgeous feet
Would fan her cheeks to keep away the heat
Would shine her shoes till she's lost in the sheen

But she's a smoke-loving girl
And I'm allergic to nicotine

Lawd now my head is in a haze
Cause of that girl and her smoke-loving ways

Blind-Date Blues

Could be he's a flower-bearing romantic
      or beer-swearing and ends up sick

Could be he's the type with a ring in one ear
      or a throwback to trousers that flare

Could be kind of cute and full of flash
      or a brute rolling in cash

Could be leather-crazy and a motorbikehound
      or dream-hazy and bookbound

Could be a smoothie meaning no hair on the head
      a ponytailed lad or lionlocked dread

Don't know which one to choose
Got me the blind-date blues

Money for
a Rainy Day

Let others save
their money
for a rainy day.
I'm saving mine
for a sunny day.

On rainy days
I want to stay
indoors and slumber.
Lose myself under
the folds of my quilt.
A case of rainy-day blues.

But on sunny days
when summer is honey
among the leaves
and there's a boogie
in my stride,
that's when I need my money.

Yeah, I put aside
a little something
for a sunny day,
so I can step out a treat
to greet the heat.

Tidy Up with Music

for Lesley

Mum says tidy up your room and do it today
But how can she tidy up without a cool dee jay

So many things to chuck in the bin
Just don't know where to begin

She can only tidy up with music
She can only tidy up with music

She promises Mum she'll make her room neat
But she must have that rapping beat

Gotta have that beat loud as she can
How else can she reach for a dustpan

She can only tidy up with music
She can only tidy up with music

She can tidy up much-much-faster
To the sound of the ghetto-blaster

Come on Mum don't be a square
When I vacuum-clean it's music I hear

She can only tidy up with music
She can only tidy up with music

So Mum's poor head will know no rest
Or that room will stay a complete mess

Nextdoor Harmony

POP UP DE MUSIC
BLAST UP DE BEAT
Who cares if the neighbours can't sleep

RAGE OUT RAP
MAKE REGGAE REIGN
Who cares if nextdoor complain

TEASE DE TREBLE
BOMB DE BASS
Who cares if floor and ceiling tremble

VOLUME IS THE WAY
STEREO THE KEY
To peace in the twentieth century

Then invite the police
for a cup of tea
AND A BLAST OF BEETHOVEN'S FIFTH SYMPHONY

Legend in Leather

My great-grandmother
is a legend in leather.
The trendiest leather ever seen.
And at eighty-four
she's the oldest queen
of the disco floor.

On her leather jacket
she'd sew badges and things
like the odd safety-pin
or treasured brooch
picked up on one of her outings
by coach.

She won't
be rocking-chair bound.
She grooves
to the funkiest sound.

The neighbours are outraged.
Why can't a great-gran act her age?
But I pray she'll always be
a legend in leather
and never fade beneath the weather.

'That will be the day,' says my great-grandmother.
'I'll even get my kicks with a walking stick.'

Poetry Jump-up

Tell me if Ah seeing right
Take a look down de street

Words dancin
words dancin
till dey sweat
words like fishes
jumpin out a net
words wild and free
joinin de poetry revelry
words back to back
words belly to belly

Come on everybody
come and join de poetry band
dis is poetry carnival
dis is poetry bacchanal
when inspiration call
take yu pen in yu hand
if yu don't have a pen
take yu pencil in yu hand
if yu don't have a pencil
what the hell
so long de feeling start to swell
just shout de poem out

Words jumpin off de page
tell me if Ah seein right
words like birds
jumpin out a cage
take a look down de street
words shakin dey waist
words shakin dey bum
words wit black skin
words wit white skin
words wit brown skin

words wit no skin at all
words huggin up words
an sayin I want to be a poem today
rhyme or no rhyme
I is a poem today
I mean to have a good time

Words feeling hot hot hot
big words feeling hot hot hot
lil words feeling hot hot hot
even sad words cant help
tappin dey toe
to de riddum of de poetry band

Dis is poetry carnival
dis is poetry bacchanal
so come on everybody
join de celebration
all yu need is plenty perspiration
an a little inspiration
plenty perspiration
an a little inspiration

What the Teacher Said When Asked: What Er We Avin for Geography, Miss?

This morning I've got too much energy
much too much for geography

I'm in a high mood
so class don't think me crude
but you can stuff latitude and longitude

I've had enough of the earth's crust
today I want to touch the clouds

Today I want to sing out loud
and tear all maps to shreds

I'm not settling for river beds
I want the sky and nothing less

Today I couldn't care if east turns west
Today I've got so much energy
I could do press-ups on the desk
but that won't take much out of me

Today I'll dance on the globe
in a rainbow robe

while you class remain seated
on your natural zone
with your pens and things
watching my contours grow wings

All right, class, see you later.
If the headmaster asks for me
say I'm a million dreaming degrees
beyond the equator

a million dreaming degrees
beyond the equator

A Party Animal

I'm a party animal.
Disco lights cast a spell.
I come out of my shell.

I'm a party animal.
When the music begins
I'm all feathers, fur and fins.

I'm a party animal.
I never miss a do.
I grunt, I purr, I buzz, I coo.

I'm a party animal.
When the night is swinging
my arms do a chimpanzee fling.

I'm a party animal.
Things may wind down when it's late
But I'm not one to flake.

Oh no, I hop, I strut, I'm all display
way past the earliest dawn of day.
Then I simply hibernate.

DJ Ghost

I'm the disco ghost
your supernatural DJ

When I was alive
I'd boogie the night away

Yeah man
I was all for rave and jive
in my cool trendy rags

And it's still a joy to see
from my position of invisibility

the girls dance around their handbags

But it's a greater joy for me
to breathe into the mike
(TESTING ONE TWO THREE)

and do a spooky rap

I even do a spooky toast
like a true streetwise disco ghost.
What a pity they can't see

my invisible chill-out cap

WICKED CRUCIAL AND ALL THAT YO

Skeletons have a night life
in case you didn't know

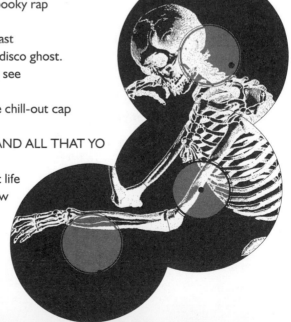

A Hello From Cello

Stroke

me

high

Stroke

me

low

with a ripple of your bow

till my plump body

begins to glow

with the O-so-sweet harmony.

Make me hum make me buzz make me drone.

Rest my slender neck beside your own.

Close me in the secret of your lap

till fall of curtain and fade of clap.

Remember my ornate toe will be curled

like a rude question mark

against the applause in your ear.

I may even whisper four-letter words

such as

Bach

Aria

Opus

When Light
and Shadow

Half-caste

Excuse me
standing on one leg
I'm half-caste

Explain yuself
wha yu mean
when yu say half-caste
yu mean when picasso
mix red an green
is a half-caste canvas/
explain yuself
wha yu mean
when yu say half-caste
yu mean when light an shadow
mix in de sky
is a half-caste weather/
well in dat case
england weather
nearly always half-caste
in fact some o dem cloud
half-caste till dem overcast
so spiteful dem dont want de sun pass
ah rass/
explain yuself
wha yu mean
when yu say half-caste
yu mean when tchaikovsky
sit down at dah piano

an mix a black key
wid a white key
is a half-caste symphony/

Explain yuself
wha yu mean
Ah listening to yu wid de keen
half of mih ear
Ah lookin at yu wid de keen
half of mih eye
an when I'm introduced to you
I'm sure you'll understand
why I offer yu half-a-hand
an when I sleep at night
I close half-a-eye
consequently when I dream
I dream half-a-dream
an when moon begin to glow
I half-caste human being
cast half-a-shadow
but yu must come back tomorrow

wid de whole of yu eye
an de whole of yu ear
an de whole of yu mind

an I will tell yu
de other half
of my story

The Howdooyoodoo

Haven't you heard
of the howdooyoodoo
howdooyoodoo?

I'm surprised
you haven't heard
of the howdooyoodoo
howdooyoodoo

Spend a day or two
in a place called England
and I'm sure you'll meet
the howdooyoodoo
howdooyoodoo

But for those of you
without a clue
the howdooyoodoo
is a creeping kind of plant
that takes you by the hand
and says howdooyoodoo
howdooyoodoo

And if by chance
you should say
I'm feeling down today
I got a tumour in my brain
and my old grandmother
keeps haemorrhaging
drops of rain
that doctors can't restrain

Then the howdooyoodoo
gets embarrassed
almost a fright
retreats into itself
and begins to wither

So upon meeting
the howdooyoodoo
this most peculiar plant
don't be alarmed
be polite
just take it by the hand
and say howdooyoodoo
howdooyoodoo
howdooyoodoo
howdooyoodoooooooooooooooooooooooooo

Tessa

*after seeing a TV programme in which Olympic gold medallist Tessa Sanderson
revealed that she had returned to Britain from her Olympic triumph to be
told by her dad about a racist letter someone had written*

Tessa

caress

the light

of the sun

kiss

the wind

with the lips

of a javelin

aim

to the glint

of stars

aim and sprint

aim and sprint

for stars

know your name

stars understand

the language

of gold

and if silence

is golden

then stars

are silence

but stars

speak wonders

wonders

foolish hands

that write foolish

letters

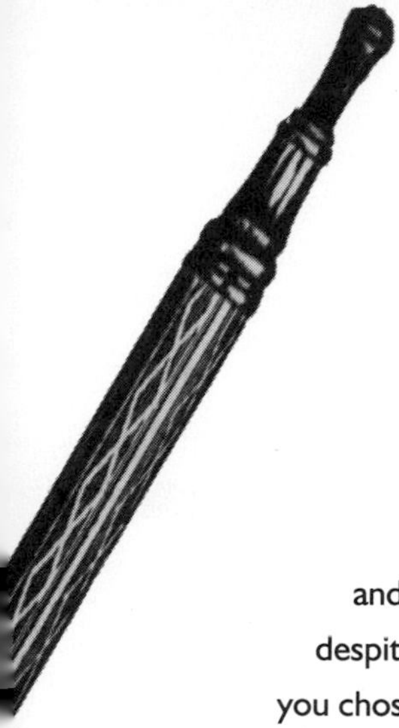

will never
begin to understand
that Britain is only an island
surrounded by water
and for that matter
an eye is an island
surrounded by tears or smiles

and you chose to smile
despite
you chose to smile

so run gal run yuh run
nah mek gold spoil ya
run gal run
run abreast of yuh vision

At Your Doorstep

The trees
where are the trees?

The birds
are now homeless

But have no fear.
The birds are planning
to build their nests
in human hair.

The rivers
where are the rivers?
Is this a nightmare?

No my friend
the homeless fish
are gasping
at your doorstep.
But why don't the humans answer?

The humans?
What humans?

Just a Thought

One day Deer, limping through the forest,
had the following thought:

I'd love to remove Man's balls
and make a perfume.
I'd rub a little behind my horns
and call it Musk.

Good thinking, said Elephant,
flashing a tusk.
I long to have a crack
at turning Man's head
into an umbrella rack.

Then Fox remarked, ever crafty:
I've heard of a wolf in sheep's clothing,
and at our next fancy-dress party
I'd give anything
to be a fox dressed up in human skin.

Bugged

We've been bugged, said Mama Bug to Papa Bug.
We bugs must be so careful how we speak.
In our conversation there's been a leak.
Must be those humans again
The ones from the telly
Doing a documentary:
A DAY IN THE LIFE OF A CREEPY-CRAWLY.

Sure we've been bugged, said Papa Bug to Mama Bug.
My instincts tell me someone's secretly
recording our bug-to-bug chat.
I swear there's a teeny-weeny
microphone somewhere in our cosy tree-flat
Could be anywhere. In the vein of a leaf
Even under the mossy cheek of a stone.
You can never tell with a microphone.

Yes, Yes, we've been bugged, said Baby Bug,
And there it is!
Pointing to the teeny-weeny microphone
disguised as a raindrop
Picking up their every word.

Well done, said Mama Bug and Papa Bug to Baby Bug.
One of these days you'll grow up to be a mighty fine Bug.

Crybaby Prime Minister

I'd love to be led
by a crybaby prime minister
who'd burst into tears
whenever people bled

I'd love to be led
by a crybaby prime minister
who'd sob and sob
for everyone without a job

I'd love to be led
by a crybaby prime minister
who'd lose all control
when told of old folks in the cold

I'd love to be led
by a crybaby prime minister
who'd whimper for a while
at the mention of nuclear missile

I'd love to be led
by a crybaby prime minister
who'd suddenly weep
for children with nowhere to sleep

I'd love to be led
by a crybaby prime minister
whose eyes would go red
when trees of the forest are felled

Yes, there's something to be said
for a nation being led
by a crybaby prime minister
who'd reach for a hanky
with a lump in the throat

Such a prime minister
might be worth a vote.

Checking Out Me History

Dem tell me
Dem tell me
Wha dem want to tell me

Bandage up me eye with me own history
Blind me to me own identity

Dem tell me bout 1066 and all dat
dem tell me bout Dick Whittington and he cat
But Toussaint L'Ouverture
no dem never tell me bout dat

Toussaint
a slave
with vision
lick back
Napoleon
battalion
and first Black
Republic born
Toussaint de thorn
to de French
Toussaint de beacon
of de Haitian Revolution

Dem tell me bout de man who discover de balloon
and de cow who jump over de moon
Dem tell me bout de dish run away with de spoon
but dem never tell me bout Nanny de maroon

Nanny
See-far woman
of mountain dream
fire-woman struggle
hopeful stream
to freedom river

Dem tell me bout Lord Nelson and Waterloo
but dem never tell me bout Shaka de great Zulu
Dem tell me bout Columbus and 1492
but what happen to de Caribs and de Arawaks too

Dem tell me bout Florence Nightingale and she lamp
and how Robin Hood used to camp
Dem tell me bout ole King Cole was a merry ole soul
but dem never tell me bout Mary Seacole

From Jamaica
she travel far
to the Crimean War
she volunteer to go
and even when de British said no
she still brave the Russian snow
a healing star
among the wounded
a yellow sunrise
to the dying

Dem tell me
Dem tell me wha dem want to tell me
But now I checking out me own history
I carving out me identity

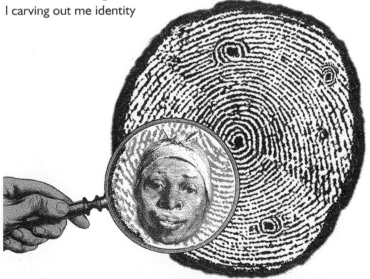

Angela Davis and Joan of Arc Rap

*from a dance drama, Talking Spirits (1991), commissioned and performed
by ADZIDO Pan-African Dance Ensemble*

Angela Davis militant walked a path of fire
She fought to lift her people higher

Joan of Arc peasant girl in a man's outfit
She led an army and that took some grit

Angela stood up for what she believed was right
Joan stood up too dressed as a knight

Both these women stood for integrity
They had a few questions for society

You couldn't call either a passive stereotype
I tell you people don't believe that hype

They looked at Joan and said there come a witch
They looked at Angela and said communist

And while the pressure was building outside
These two women listened to the voice inside

Now Joan was white and Angela black
Both followed their conscience no looking back

Racism is a monster with an ugly grin
And religious bigots try to scare you with sin

Could be the Inquisition or the Ku Klux Klan
Could be a skinhead or a drunken old man

A girl's got to do what a girl's got to do
I'm talking to the Joan and Angela in you

And if you don't like my rap close your mind
Like Angela said Lift the people while you climb

Cowboy Movies

On cowboy movies
they show you Indians as baddies
and cowboys as goodies
but think again please.
Who disturb de dreams
of de sleeping wigwam
who come with de guns
going blam blam blam?
Think again please

One Question from a Bullet

I want to give up being a bullet
I've been a bullet too long

I want to be an innocent coin
in the hand of a child
and be squeezed through the slot
of a bubblegum machine

I want to give up being a bullet
I've been a bullet too long

I want to be a good luck seed
lying idle in somebody's pocket
or some ordinary little stone
on the way to becoming an earring
or just lying there unknown
among a crowd of other ordinary stones

I want to give up being a bullet
I've been a bullet too long

The question is
Can you give up being a killer?

Limbo Dancer at Immigration

It was always the same
at every border/ at every frontier/
at every port/ at every airport/
                    of every metropolis

The same hassle
from authorities

the same battle
with bureaucrats

a bunch of official cats
ready to scratch

looking limbo dancer up & down
scrutinizing passport with a frown

COUNTRY OF ORIGIN: SLAVESHIP

Never heard of that one
the authorities sniggered

Suppose you got here on a banana boat
the authorities sniggered

More likely a spaceship
the authorities sniggered

Slaveship/ spaceship/ Pan Am/ British Airways/ Air France
It's all the same
smiled the limbo dancer

Now don't give us any of your lip
the authorities sniggered

ANY IDENTIFYING MARKS?

And when limbo dancer showed them sparks
of vision in eyes that held rivers
                        it meant nothing to them

And when limbo dancer held up hands
that told a tale of nails
                        it meant nothing to them

And when limbo dancer offered a neck
that bore the brunt of countless lynchings
                        it meant nothing to them

And when limbo dancer revealed ankles
bruised with the memory of chains
                        it meant nothing to them

So limbo dancer bent over backwards
                        & danced
                        & danced
                        & danced

until from every limb
flowed a trail of red

& what the authorities thought
was a trail of blood

was only spilt duty-free wine

so limbo dancer smiled
saying I have nothing to declare

& to the sound of drum disappeared

I'd Like to Squeeze

Secret

Tell me your secret.
I promise not to tell.
I'll guard it safely at the bottom of a well.

Tell me your secret
Tell me, tell me, please.
I won't breathe a word, not even to the bees.

Tell me your secret.
It will be a pebble in my mouth.
Not even the sea can make me spit it out.

Song on Skates

They had a date
at the skating rink

He was late
and she was late

But so what
it didn't matter

They kept the date
at the skating rink

Fun was a brink
for rolling over

And at sixteen
the whole world seemed pink

A Date with Spring

Got a date with Spring
Got to look me best.
Of all the trees
I'll be the smartest dressed.

Perfumed breeze
behind me ear.
Pollen accessories
all in place.
Raindrop moisturizer
for me face.
Sunlight tints
to spruce up the hair.

What's the good of being a tree
if you can't flaunt your beauty?

Winter, I was naked.
Exposed as can be.
Me wardrobe took off
with the wind.
Life was a frosty slumber.
Now, Spring, here I come.
Can't wait to slip in
to me little green number.

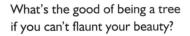

I Never Let on

LIPSTICK –
a new-found flame
to light up a lip

MASCARA –
a fluttering veil
to moth up an eyelash

TIGHTS –
as fishnet as they come
to mystify a thigh

Call me a tart. I don't mind.
I just love it when boys sigh

and stammer my name –
though I never let on
I'm skilled in the art

of KICK-BOXING.

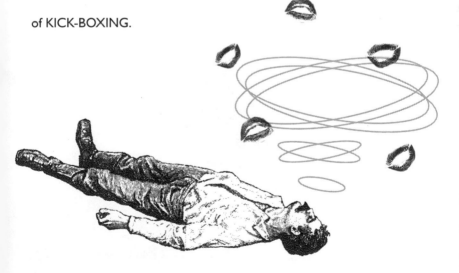

Telephone

The telephone
is a creature
that springs

It sleeps
as lightly
as a cat
and leaps
on you
when your back
is turned

I used to think
it a pest
how it buzzes
and rings

But now
miles from you

I place
this creature
to my ear

and my heart sings

On the Disco Floor

Laser beams
    make dreams
    of my head

Smoke lights
    ferriswheel
    down my eyes

and I feel
    the night
    is a horse

we're riding
    to nowhere

But if the feeling
    is all right
    with you
    it's all right
    with me

    So hold tight
    hold the mane
    of midnight

and kiss me again

Puppy Love

for Yansan

We yapped for hours on the telephone.
Nice nothings whispered in teasy tones.
Smelt each other across the miles
from Brighton to San Francisco.
Collect. Reverse charges. Mum and Dad wouldn't know.
He's missing me. I miss him. Blow a long-distance kiss.
We wagged our teenage tongues in wicked bliss.
GET OFF THAT PHONE. WE'LL HAVE A MASSIVE BILL.
Parents' fears were nagging fleas in our ears.
We barked delight at the moon of sweet sixteen.
Bit the bone of thrills between laughter and tears.
Licked longing from the back of absence. Didn't have a care.
Chased the tails of moments when petting was magic.
So what if they called it puppy love?
At least, for a while, happiness howled.

Hairstyle

What about my hairstyle?
On my head I carry
a phosphorescent porcupine
but it's mine it's mine
and if you don't like my head
you can drop dead

What about my hairstyle?
On my head I bear a mane
of flaming dreadlocks
sometimes hidden by the red gold and green
but flaming all the same
with I-rie pride of Africa.
Know what I mean?

What about my hairstyle?
On my head I wear
a Mohican rainbow
that makes me glow.
I know some eyebrows go
up in despair
but it's my hair it's my hair

What about my hairstyle?
On my head I show a crown
of incandescent candy floss.
Who cares if some people frown
and say, 'young people are lost'
At least me mum doesn't get on me back
She says, 'I suppose you're only young once'

What about my hairstyle?
On my head I have whispers
of braided beads
Me mum says she wouldn't have the patience
But these beads are in no hurry
I tell them my needs
They listen to the song inside of me

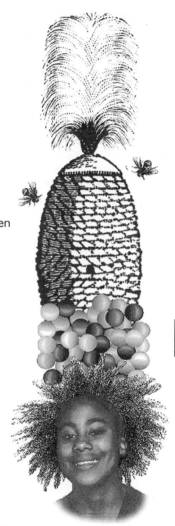

Way-out Mum Way-out Dad

Mum dyes her hair incandescent green
and paints her nails
a shade of midnight blue.

Dad wears a ponytail, listens to Cream
and goes on about a book
called The Tao Of Pooh.

What do you do when your parents are so liberal
they pinch your rap and heavy metal
and don't mind a nosering or tattoo?

It embarrasses me to tell,
but when their bedroom gives off that incense smell,
I know – I just know – they're smooching
and carrying on to a small Tibetan bell.

Oh what do you do with a mum and dad
who're so cool, streetwise and hip to the scene,
they make me feel like a has-been
and I'm only fourteen.

They've given me nothing
against which I can rebel.
Just to annoy them I'll grow up
sweet and straight as an angel.

Spell to Banish a Pimple

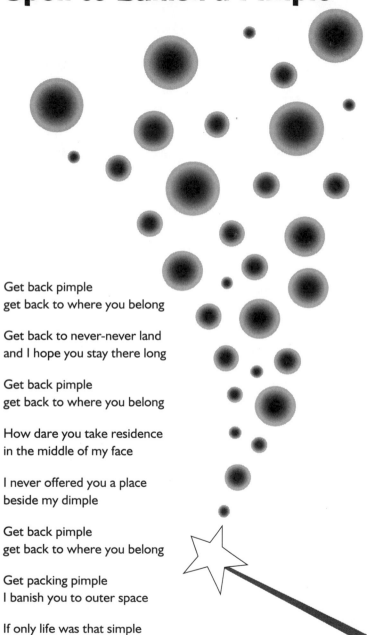

Get back pimple
get back to where you belong

Get back to never-never land
and I hope you stay there long

Get back pimple
get back to where you belong

How dare you take residence
in the middle of my face

I never offered you a place
beside my dimple

Get back pimple
get back to where you belong

Get packing pimple
I banish you to outer space

If only life was that simple

In a Concrete Jungle Calypso

Tarzan in a concrete jungle
this might give you a shock
Tarzan in a concrete jungle
swinging from highrise tower block

Tarzan in a concrete jungle
jogging to keep in shape
Tarzan in a concrete jungle
competing with an ape

Tarzan in a concrete jungle
can't find no tiger to fight
Tarzan in a concrete jungle
battling with a traffic light

Tarzan in a concrete jungle
dancing with Jane at disco
Tarzan in a concrete jungle
acting the part of hero

Tarzan in a concrete jungle
macho man with chimpanzee
Tarzan in a concrete jungle
hunting for a wimpy

Tarzan in a concrete jungle
calling out for B-O-Yyyyyyy
Tarzan in a concrete jungle
lost among the unemployed

Tarzan in a concrete jungle
get me out of here by hook or crook
Tarzan in a concrete jungle
please put me back in a comic book

AAAaaaaAAAAAaaa!!!

Zoomtime for Paul

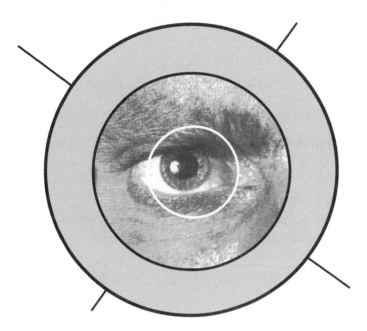

My stepfather thinks I'm useless.
He says I can't tell east from west.
Shouldn't even dream of a driving test.

Says I've got two left feet.
If I was face to face with goal
I'd most likely blunder the ball.

If I was three rungs up a ladder
He thinks I'd probably fall.
And he wouldn't trust me with a hammer.

My stepfather thinks I'm useless.
What I haven't told him is this:
At photography I'm simply the best.

One day I'll zoom in on my stepfather
with a fast film and double exposure.
Maybe he'd be so proud he'd be speechless.

A Chat-up Line

Talking to girls turns me to jelly.
There's a frog in my throat
and a butterfly in my belly.

I've dipped into magazine sex guides
to pick up a few tips
but nothing seems to unfreeze my lips.

I'll seek the aid of the divine
or a correspondence course
all for the sake of a chat-up line.

Why do I shift from foot to foot
and go all awkward?
Why can't I manage a single word?

Girls makes my sinews soften.
My eyes are rooted to the ceiling.
I can't even utter 'Do you come here often?'

Now, if I was from the Wodaabe tribe
I'd roll my eye like a small black moon.
That would surely make some girl swoon.

If I was a knight of chivalry
I'd challenge a rival to a duel.
My shining sword will win her heart's jewel.

If I was a sumo wrestler
I'd have no need of words.
My telling bulk would impress her.

Oh is there no hope for guys like me?
I've even turned for help
from a TV wildlife documentary.

Yes, I'd exchange places with pheasant or goose
only to parade my plumage, fan out my tail.
My strutting will succeed where words fail.

Meanwhile, a chat-up line is a monumental task,
though a certain girl once said to me
'I like boys like you. So shy and afraid to ask.'

Behold My Pen

Behold my pen
my pen is a friend
that cries
blue tears
on the cheek
of a page

Behold my pen
my pen is a friend
that flies
across the cloud
of a page

Behold my pen
my pen is a friend
that spies
a face
in the mirror
of a page

Behold my pen
my pen is a friend
that sometimes
speaks truth
sometimes lies

How do I dare erase
the footprints of my friend?

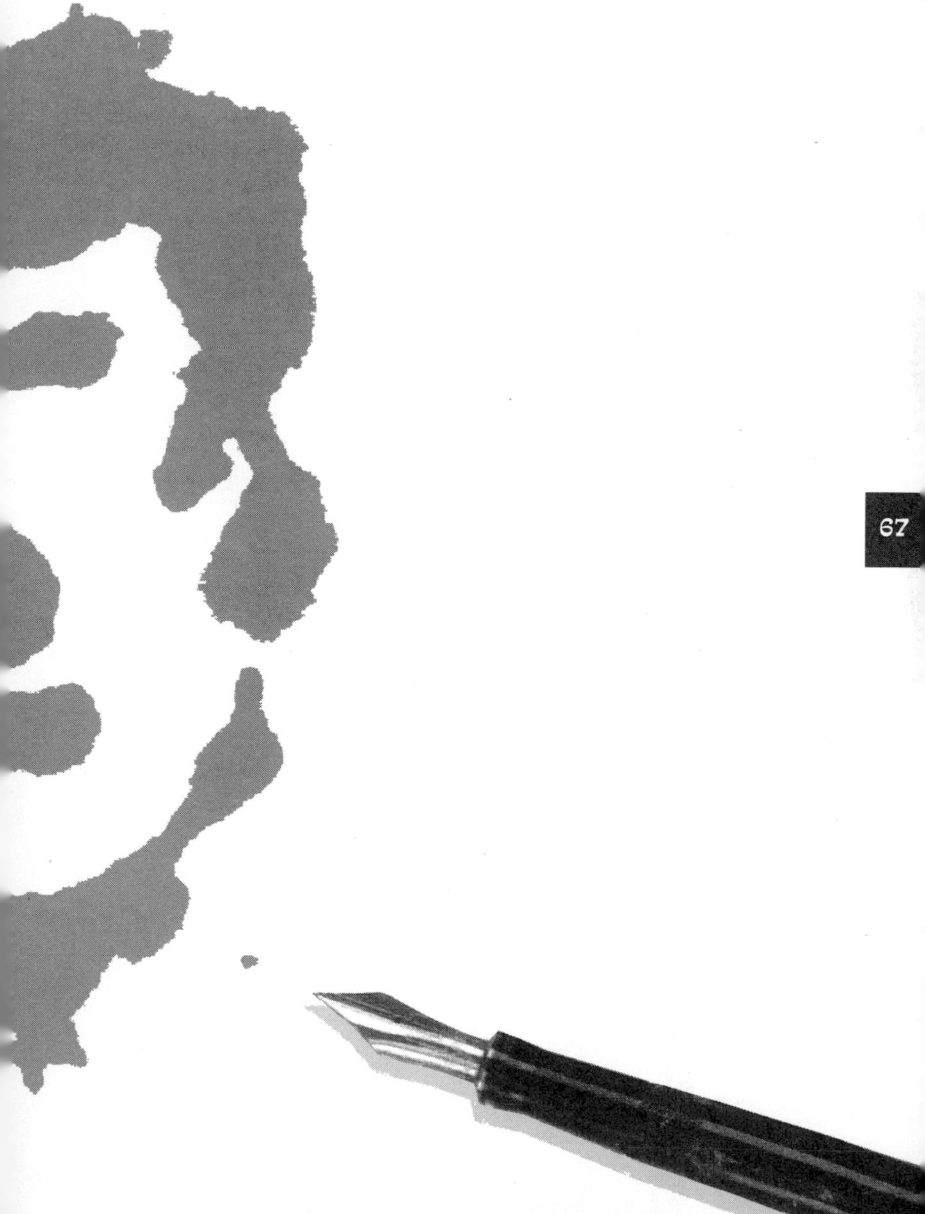

PC Poet

'Why don't you be
a policeman
instead of a poet?'
the little girl asked

Well, you see,
I chose to be
a poet

but I suppose I am
a kind of policeman

I prefer
to chase a word
for speeding

interrogate
a sentence

for parking
on a dotted line

charge an image
for illicit flight
of fancy

arrest a poem
for assaulting me
in the dead of night

and I too
have the power
to force a confession
out of a flower

Know what I mean?
The only difference
is I suppose
paper does not bleed

Tough Guy

There's a tear trying to tiptoe
towards the edge of your eye tough guy
there's a tear leaning
in the direction of your eye
towards the rim of your eye tough guy

What's the matter tough guy

Why do you push it down
with the palm of your ego

A tear wouldn't bruise your eyelid

Maybe tough guy when you were a kid
they told you little boys don't cry
didn't you ever see your daddy peeling onions?

Your hands can talk to steel and batteries
but can't bear to deal
with the weight of a leaf

Tough luck tough guy
have a good cry

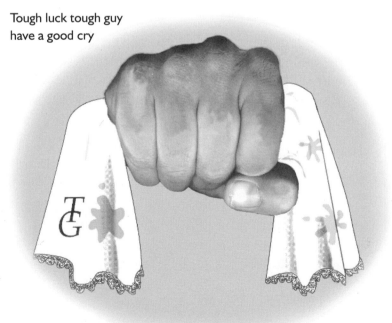

Verdict

EXHIBIT A

The first photograph
shows a pair of hands
so beautifully groomed
they look almost pure.
Those were the hands
that held the knife
that did the stabbing.
Those the hands that took a life.

EXHIBIT B

The second photograph
shows another pair of hands
so heavily gnarled
almost as hard as bark.
Those were the hands
that dug the hole to plant
a seed inside the earth.
Those the hands that make things grow.

EXHIBIT C

The third photograph
shows a man without hands.
Crippled from birth
he types poems with his toes.
Balances soup between his knees.
Caresses a woman with his ankles.
Possesses such dexterity
he finds hands unnecessary.

Ladies and gentlemen
before reaching a decision
I beg you to ponder
on the nature of beauty
and the relevance of hands.

Onset

Voice breaking
on the pebbly shore
of a teenage tongue

Pimples staking
claim to the territory
of a puzzled face

Hair suggesting itself
in the purse of your arm
and pubic patch

Puppy fat nesting
in the branch of your jeans
and careers make you scared

And you wait for the phone to ring
as Big Brother boasts budding beard
and granny smith biceps

Little does he know
in the pit of your stomach
you can hear the drum of womanhood roll

And your mum repeats
exactly what she herself was told
when pads and flushes first marked her month:

'Watch out now what you do with boys.'

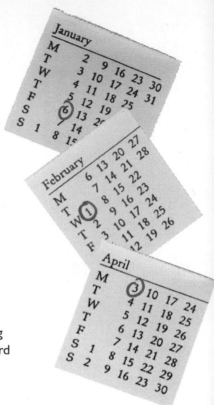

I'd Like to Squeeze

I'd like to squeeze this round world
into a new shape

I'd like to squeeze this round world
like a tube of toothpaste

I'd like to squeeze this world
fair and square

I'd like to squeeze it and squeeze it
till everybody had an equal share

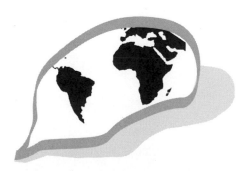

74

God in Blue Denims

The Storyteller's Cup

Listen all and listen well.

With this cup
I drank an ancient mead
and saw a dragon bleed.

With this cup
I toasted to the sky
and a god flew in my eye.

With this cup
I sipped a bitter brew
and saw the sun turn blue.

With this cup
I swigged from a holy well
and heard the sea inside a bell.

Drink from this cup, you who will,
And you'll never be short of a tale to tell.

Seven New Year Resolutions

To harvest every morning
with cool-cropping YES

To jump every hurdle
with wind-topping ease

To challenge every mind
with open-popping question

To cherish every kiss
with heart-stopping thrill

To walk every street
with hip-hopping stride

To welcome every sleep
with body-flopping bliss

Simply to wake to the world
with baby-bopping eyes

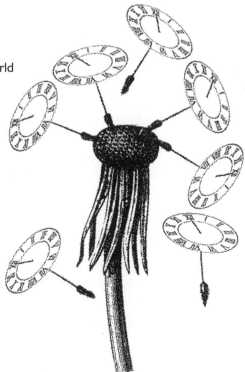

Who Are You?

I am the kryptonite
that gave Superman a fright
  and reduced to naught his might

I am the arrow
that found the heel of Achilles
  and brought his chariot low

I am the spindle
that pricked a maiden's finger
  and confined her in slumber

I am the mistletoe
that became a dart
  and pierced poor Balder's heart

And you, sir, who are you?

I am the Joker in the pack.
 The straw
  that will break the camel's back

Fisherman Chant

Sister river
Brother river
Mother river
Father river
O life giver
O life taker
O friend river
What have you
in store
for a poor
fisherman
today?

From my boat
I cast my net
to your heart
O friend river
and I hope
you return it
gleaming with silver
O friend river

Sister river
Brother river
Mother river
Father river
O life giver
O life taker
O friend river
What have you
in store
for a poor
fisherman
today?

God in Blue Denims

When the world looks grim
Imagine God in blue denims
patches and all,
badge pinned
like a fallen star.

When the world looks grim
Imagine God in blue denims
divinely zipped,
and note the holy hip
moving over mountain
in a shower of light.

That's right.
When the world looks grim
Imagine God in blue denims

striding the air
in unisexual flair

grooving to the galactic beat.

Five Deities

1. The god of pimples
is a raspberryeyed
tonguetied schemer.

He sits on an Olympus
of scabs and pustules
surrounded by his eloquent
blotchhead advisers

He awaits the moment
     to ambush
the unsuspecting adolescent.

Then one day when you're smartly
dressed and feeling cheeky,
he'll give the move-in orders
     to his army of acne

2. The god of the ghettoblaster
cannot speak a word of Greek
but he surveys the underground
swinging his chariot of sound.

He observes from far the frantic ratrace.
Cares not for the laws of silence
or the formality of a briefcase.

The god of the ghettoblaster
moves at his own music-driven pace
sending his highvoltage thunderbolt
into the eardrums of puny mortals.

3. The goddess of trainers
is a fleetfooted
maker of tracks to far-out and beyond.

She's never heard of high-tech or low-tech.
She strides bedecked
in the whirlwind
of her Atalanta steps.

The goddess of trainers
beckons
an infinity of directions.

4. The god of the skateboard
is a surfer
on road waves

a T-shirt Poseidon
in the Saturday morning centre of town.
Pavements are his kingdom.

With an up
and a down
and a fancy
wheel around

Who dares deny him attention?

5. The goddess of the personal stereo
is a ruler of the earhive.
Queen Bee amplified.

And a thousand
funky bees
obey her electronic command.

Soon they will fill the air with a crackling fuzz
and the goddess of the personal stereo
will glory in the beat of the buzz ... the buzz ...

There Was This Girl Who Liked Her Boys in Alphabetical Order

ADAM
She thought kind of naïve.
He always kept an apple up his sleeve.

BAUDELAIRE
Sent her evil flowers for Valentine
And filled her shoes with wine.

CATULLUS
Spoke to her in Latin, a language supposed to be dead.
But he made some living noises and pointed to the bed.

DARWIN
Behaved like a right old monkey. Good for a laugh
Especially when he did his impression of a short-neck giraffe.

EINSTEIN
Chatted her up at an all-night party. Said something about 'atom!'
But the music was so loud, she thought he said 'bottom'.

FREDDIE
Was mercurial. The fastest guy she ever seen.
But he turned out to be a queen.

GAGARIN
Said I'll take you to the moon
Even if it means travelling there in a balloon.

HANNIBAL
Said forget the moon. Try my elephant. Hop on.
Test these biceps. Touch these pecs. Feel how strong.

IMHOTEP
Completely bald. Looked divine. And dandruff-free.
One day, he said, I'll design a pyramid just for you and me.

JIMI
Said my guitar's groovy, my hair's wild,
Won't you be my voodoo child?

KRISHNA
Had a thing about milkmaids who were cute.
They met at classes for flute.

LEONARDO
Said I'll do you a statue. Marble. Bronze. You choose.
She said thank you, but how about a pair of platform shoes?

MOZART
Believe it or not, once called her a tart
As if that was the way to win her heart.

NARCISSUS
Wore tight-fitting jeans and trendy clothes
Couldn't stop looking at himself in shop windows.

ODYSSEUS
Could never remember her name. Kept calling her Penelope
And sending her postcards from across the sea.

PYTHAGORAS
Helped her with her maths homework, which was cool.
But when he compared her eyes to triangles she thought him a fool.

QUIXOTE
Approached her on a battered horse like some shining knight.
She wondered why he never considered a motorbike.

RASPUTIN
Well, he was funny. Kept wiggling a little finger before her eyes,
Hoping she'd be hypnotized. At least he tried.

SOLOMON
Too clever for his own good. A wizard at computers and video games.
He still fancies her but he's just an 'old flame'.

TARZAN
Tried to impress her with a swinging yodelling trick.
But she couldn't stand his taste in music.

URASHIMA
Promised her a palace beneath the waves. A sea princess!
Now he's back in Japan and she's misplaced his address.

VAN GOGH
Asked to borrow her yellow felt pen
Then drew her a sunflower signed Your ever friend.

WINKLE

Always showed up late for a date, a miles-away smirk on his face.
He'd fall asleep at a movie, half-way through a car chase.

XOCHIPILLI
Made her think of exotic flowers and birds of bright feathers.
Unfortunately, he was allergic to her mohair sweaters.

YU
Wanted to save the planet. Be a caring engineer.
Said she danced like water through air.

ZEKE
Who called her his heaven and hell
And once covered her hair in bluebells.

(Poor Zeke, who didn't like his name Ezekiel,
And wrote her that one letter from Israel.)

The Hurt Boy and the Birds

The hurt boy talked to the birds
and fed them the crumbs of his heart.

It was not easy to find the words
for secrets he hid under his skin.
The hurt boy spoke of a bully's fist
that made his face a bruised moon –
his spectacles stamped to ruin.

It was not easy to find the words
for things that nightly hissed
as if his pillow was a hideaway for creepy-crawlies –
the note sent to the girl he fancied
held high in mockery.

But the hurt boy talked to the birds
and their feathers gave him welcome –

Their wings taught him new ways to become.

Aggro and Nag

When Aggro and Nag
make life a drag
I build a peanutbutter sandwich
and close my bedroom door

Mum and Dad think it's untidy
but in my room I find me
among planets of records
and CD constellations.
In my room I'm lord
of the galaxy.

To deal with Aggro and Nag
Mum and Dad resort to a fag.
I build a peanutbutter sandwich
and close my bedroom door

Sometimes I lose myself
in one of my books
which Mum and Dad say
are 'in disarray'.
But to me my books
are my pyramid of pages
– my bridgeway
to distant ages

As for those denims
dismissed as a 'pile'
they're unwashed clouds
that turn my floor to sky.

My room's untidy? Says who?
When Aggro and Nag
are getting to my bag
You know what I do, don't you?

Build a peanutbutter sandwich
four storeys high.
Close my bedroom door and fly.

In My New Trainers

I'll walk the streets of Saturday

and leave my down-days behind

The whole world will stare

at the flashing fish of my feet

I'll step on waves of air

I'll hip I'll hop

to a hidden beat

Wherever I go

good vibes will flow

I'll follow the sideways

and byways of the universe

where friendly encounters

are flowers disguised

Believe me

I'll make the pavements billow

till cobblestones are stars

and streets are skies

I'll greet the birthday

in every stranger's eyes

Rainbow

When you see
de rainbow
you know
God know
wha he doing –
one big smile
across the sky –
I tell you
God got style
the man got style

When you see
raincloud pass
and de rainbow
make a show
I tell you
is God doing
limbo
the man doing
limbo

But sometimes
you know
when I see
de rainbow
so full of glow
& curving
like she bearing child
I does want know
if God
ain't a woman

If that is so
the woman got style
man she got style

Rebel Heart

A rebel
fell
from grace of sky
because he dared
to ask the question WHY

A rebel
broke
the bread of hope
and spoke
no word of lie
yet accusing mouths
sneered CRUCIFY

A rebel
stood
on burning ground
and braved
the torturers' flame.
She looked them in the eye
and betrayed
not a single name
though the hooded ones
declared DIE

O rebel heart in history's cage
teach us
how to hold our ground and FLY

First Black Man in S p a c e

Afro-Cuban cosmonaut, thirty-eight-year-old Arnaldo Tamayo Mendez, became the first black man in space as part of the two-man crew of the USSR spacecraft, Soyuz 38 (from a news release in Caribbean Contact, *October 1980).*

Others before him had gone
and come back
with their token
of moonrock
had planted their flag
and spoken
of the absence of gravity
the lightness of the body
that strange-dimensional sensation
of spacesuit foetus
floating on moondust
a goldfish capsuled
in galactic aquarium
with possible pebbles of uranium

But no one had prepared him for this
the booklets and leaflets
had said nothing of this
No the intensive briefing
had not prepared him for a meeting
with God face to face.
The press had hailed him
a national hero
an honour to the nation
a first for his race
a revolutionary breakthrough
but of this not a single clue.
Nothing about meeting
with God face to face
in outer space

Not one word
that God would be black
more so a woman
and would greet him
not with a coke and hamburger
saying 'Geewhizz guy you made it'
but would embrace him
as a long-lost brother
of her race
would utter his name
offering him a cup
of maté tea
after the long journey
would say 'Compañero a la luna bienvenido'
Wait till this gets back
to Moscow
or worse still Cape Canaveral

They won't believe the satellite photo

Spell to Bring the Boy

Eye of mahogany
Hair of palm tree
Boy I fancy
Come to me

Legs of quicksilver
Walk of a river
Boy I'm hot for
The one I'm after

Come to my corner
Come to my corner
We'll spend our days
In kisses and laughter

So cool yet so shy
I'll show you the secret
behind the mirror.
A ladder to the sky.

Spell to Bring the Girl

The girl who's rare
as a gift of black pearl

The girl who glows
over my homework gloom
What a girl what a girl
The one whose face
invades my room
and turns my sleep to sheep

The girl who's rare
as a gift of black pearl
The one who transforms the air
If I dare dare
knock at her door
Will she be my friend
Be my friend and more

She on her bike
I on my feet
What will I say when we meet?

Shak-Shak Girl

SHAK-SHAK GIRL SHE SHAKE-SHAKE-SHAKE SHE SHAK-SHAK
She shake it at wedding
She shake it at wake
She shake it at house-warming
And round a birthday cake

SHAK-SHAK GIRL SHE SHAKE-SHAKE-SHAKE SHE SHAK-SHAK
She shake it low
She shake it high
She shake it earth
She shake it sky
She shake it on a crick-crak storytelling night
And to keep away the evil eye

SHAK-SHAK GIRL SHE SHAKE-SHAKE-SHAKE SHE SHAK-SHAK
She shake it at ring-play
She shake it at harvest-day
She shake it at christening
when baby name blessed
She shake it east
She shake it west
She shake it with ancestral zest
till the moon turn Mother Hen
and the stars dance
like chickens possessed.

Saga Boy

Saga Boy
him have bragga in him talk

Saga Boy
him have swagga in him walk

Saga Boy
him have suga in him smile

Saga Boy
him have raga in him style

But underneath / him bragga
/ him swagga
/ him suga
/ him raga

Saga Boy
know how dem dagga
of prejudice pierce deep

Saga Boy
dreaming of rainbow
over highrise estate

Saga Boy
wishing him and him girlfriend
could walk to the end of morning
and like Martin Luther King
that the world would sing
a new non-violence song.

Little Blue Mini

for Brigit

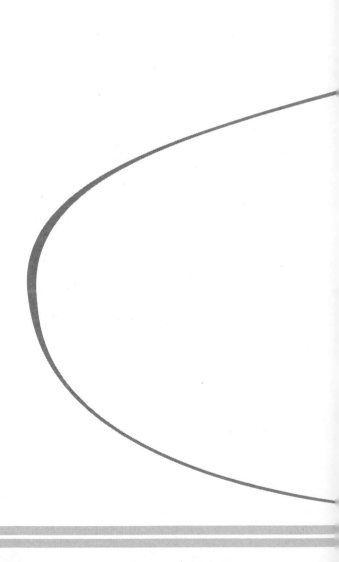

FROM ON HIGH
it's a scarab
on the shoulder
of the motorway.
In a traffic jam it's a cheeky crab
inching its way towards an opening.
And when a parking place
is heaven-sent and beckoning
Who will be first to spot that welcome space
as if reserved by some lucky star?
Who else but her little blue car
her four wheel chaperone.

Between the Cradle and the Disco

What happened between
the cradle and the disco?
Tell me where did childhood go?

I wanted to dance
but my teddy bear said no
so I threw him
out of yesterday's window

What happened between
the cradle and the disco?
Tell me where did childhood go?

I looked for clues
among my old jigsaw
but the pieces didn't fit.
I was in a hurry to be a hit

What happened between
the cradle and the disco?
Tell me where did childhood go?

I followed the laser star
but my lego ladder
didn't take me far.
So I laced up my trainers
with fingers of flight
and became the centre
of the clubbing light.

What happened between
the cradle and the disco?
Tell me where did childhood go?

Postman Pat and Charlotte's Web
are beneath the old toybox.
They didn't make it
to the top of the pops.
And now it's too late
to fiddle the clocks

What happened between
the cradle and the disco?
Tell me where did childhood go?

Into the Unknown

Like a bird
that has flown
Like a tree
that has grown

Like a cathedral
rising from
a prison of stone
Like a soul
flying from
a house of bone

I will leap
into the unknown

Calling my life my own

Notes

Hairstyle
(Page 59)
I-RIE: Greeting associated with Rastafari in the sense of 'cool' and 'highest'.

Who Are You?
(Page 78)

ACHILLES: Greek warrior killed by a poisoned arrow in his heel, his vulnerable spot.

BALDER: Norse god killed by a mistletoe sprig.

There Was This Girl Who Liked Her Boys in Alphabetical Order
(Page 84)

ADAM: Eve's mate in the biblical Garden of Eden. The Hebrew word for ground (*adamah*) is similar to that for man (Adam). They both ate the proverbial apple.

BAUDELAIRE (CHARLES) 1821–67: Dandy, rebellious nineteenth-century French poet whose most famous work is 'Les Fleurs du Mal' (The Flowers of Evil).

CATULLUS: Latin poet, probably born in 84 BC, noted for his pungent epigrams and passionate love poems.

DARWIN (CHARLES) 1809–82: English naturalist whose book *The Origin of Species* created a stir when he advanced the theory of evolution.

EINSTEIN (ALBERT) 1879–1955: German-born physicist noted for his theory of relativity. Awarded the Nobel prize for physics in 1921.

FREDDIE (MERCURY) 1946–91: Legendary performer/lead singer with rock group Queen.

GAGARIN (YURI) 1934–68: Soviet cosmonaut who became the first man in space on 12 April 1961.

HANNIBAL 247–182 BC: Carthaginian general who crossed the Alps with an army and elephants to defeat the Romans.

IMHOTEP: Egyptian high priest. Architect of the famous step pyramid at Saqqara (c.2620 BC) considered a 'stairway to heaven'.

JIMI (HENDRIX) 1942–70: Legendary US rock guitarist and singer whose innovations on the guitar became iconic of the sixties.

KRISHNA: One of the incarnations of the Hindu god VISHNU. Charming tales are told of the flute-playing cowherd Krishna and his love for the cowgirl RADHA.

LEONARDO (DA VINCI) 1452–1519: Italian artist, scientist, philosopher, inventor, engineer, who also painted the *Mona Lisa*.

MOZART (WOLFGANG AMADEUS) 1756–91: Austrian composer and child prodigy whose operas include *The Marriage of Figaro*.

NARCISSUS: Beautiful youth who, in Greek mythology, falls in love with his own reflection in a pool of water. He was changed into a flower that bears his name.

ODYSSEUS: Wandering hero of Homer's epic poem. After a series of storm-ridden adventures, he returns to his wife, Penelope.

PYTHAGORAS: Greek mathematician associated with Pythagoras' theorem in geometry.

QUIXOTE (DON): The lean knight on his hungry horse from the classic story by sixteenth-century Spanish novelist Miguel de Cervantes.

RASPUTIN (GRIGORI) ?1871–1916: Siberian peasant monk who wielded great influence with the Russian aristocracy. Associated with sexual occult.

SOLOMON: King of Israel credited in the Bible with great wisdom and an equally great number of wives.

TARZAN: Tree-swinging hero of Tarzan movies. From a series of stories by E.R. Burroughs.

URASHIMA: Young fisherman of Japanese legend. Marries a sea-maiden and lives in a palace beneath the waves. All doesn't end happily ever after.

VAN GOGH (VINCENT) 1853–90: Dutch painter noted for his emotive use of colour as in his famous sunflower series.

WINKLE (RIP VAN): Washington Irving's story (1820) of a man who falls asleep for twenty years after drinking a beverage offered by dwarfs.

XOCHIPILLI: Aztec flower god of ancient Mexico.

YU: Chinese engineer who, according to legend, gave up his family for thirteen years in order to help control the great northern floods. Also founded the first dynasty.

ZEKE (EZEKIEL): Old Testament Hebrew prophet.

Index of First Lines

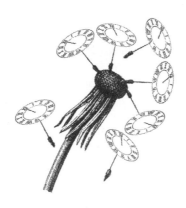

ACKNOWLEDGEMENTS

'At Your Doorstep' from *Give Me Shelter*, compiled by Michael Rosen, published by The Bodley Head 1991; 'Checking Out Me History' from *New Angles Book 2*, a selection of new and original poetry, edited by John Foster, published by Oxford University Press 1987; 'Cowboy Movies' from *Ten Golden Years*, a collection of new verse illustrated by ten Mother Goose Award winners, published by Walker Books Ltd 1989; 'First Black Man in Space' from *Angels of Fire*, an anthology of radical poetry from the 1980s, edited by Sylvia Paskin, Jay Ramsay and Jeremy Silver, published by Chatto and Windus 1986; 'Fisherman Chant' from *You'll Love This Stuff*, edited by Morag Styles, published by Cambridge University Press 1986; 'Hairstyle' from *New Angles Book 2*, a selection of new and original po-etry, edited by John Foster, published by Oxford University Press 1987; 'Half-caste' from *Black British Section – The New British Poetry*, edited by Fred D'Aguiar, published by Paladin 1988; 'The Howdooyoodoo' from *New Angles Book 2*, a selection of new and original poetry, edited by John Foster, published by Oxford University Press 1987; 'I'd Like to Squeeze' from *You'll Love This Stuff*, edited by Morag Styles, published by Cambridge University Press 1986; 'Limbo Dancer at Immigration' from *Limbo Dancer in Dark Glasses*, published by Greenheart 1983 (self-published); 'On the Disco Floor' from *New Angles Book 1*, a selection of new and original poetry, edited by John Foster, published by Oxford University Press 1987; 'One Question from a Bullet' from *Mangoes and Bullets*, selected by John Agard, published by Serpent's Tail 1990; 'Poetry Jump-up' from *You'll Love This Stuff*, edited by Morag Styles, published by Cambridge University Press 1986; 'Rainbow' from *Mangoes and Bullets*, selected by John Agard, published by Serpent's Tail 1990; 'Spell to Banish a Pimple' from *Life Doesn't Frighten Me At All*, compiled by John Agard, published by Heinemann; 'Tessa' from *One for Blair*, an anthology of poems for young people, edited by Chris Searle, published by Young World Books 1989; 'Tough Guy' from *Mangoes and Bullets*, selected by John Agard, published by Serpent's Tail 1990; 'What the Teacher Said When Asked: What Er We Avin for Geography, Miss?' from *Can I Buy a Slice of Sky?*, edited by Grace Nichols, published by Blackie and Son Ltd 1991.